Slices of Life

Slices of Life

The Drama of God's Grace in Poem and Portrait

Rev. Dr. Albert J. D. Walsh

with Patrick Lee Walsh

RESOURCE *Publications* · Eugene, Oregon

SLICES OF LIFE
The Drama of God's Grace in Poem and Portrait

Resource Publications
An Imprint of Wipf and Stock Publishers
199 W. 8th Ave., Suite 3
Eugene, OR 97401
www.wipfandstock.com

ISBN 13: 978-61097-971-9
Manufactured in the U.S.A.

For those who have inspired my life in Christ
Soli Deo Gloria

"He shines in all that's fair."

Contents

Contents

Author's Foreword

FOR SOME twenty-six years I have sensed that the reflective, meditative reading of the Bible produces a harvest of spiritual insights when the imagination is given, freely and in faith, to the guidance and direction of the Holy Spirit. I make no claim to this being a novel approach to the Bible, as the writings of Ignatius, Origin, and others offer the same and with far greater eloquence. In fact, this method of biblical reflection resonates with the ancient practice of *lectio divina*. Because the individual believer cannot extract himself or herself from the *bond* formed with the "body of Christ," and just because that same "body" was given birth and continues to be sustained by "one Lord, one faith, one baptism, one God and Father" of all, it only stands to reason that this practice of biblical reflection does not promote an individual, private, or relativistic approach to scriptural engagement and comprehension.

However, I would argue that the so-called *historical-critical* approach to the Bible, even though providing a substantial body of extremely helpful material for understanding scriptural texts at a number of levels has also, perhaps inadvertently, led to a type of one-sidedness in the approach to biblical engagement. The productive employment of what I once heard another call *faithful-imagination* in biblical study has been either held in suspicion or denied a reasonable place in the reflective process. I have no desire to discredit the *historical-critical* approach to engagement with the Bible—whether for the pastor setting about the task of sermon preparation or the lay person preparing a lesson to be taught in a setting of Christian education. I have found that the limitations of this particular method readily become evident when the attempt is to enter a biblical text at a deeper level, seeking *spiritual fruit to feed the heart, soul, and mind.*

Over the years I have developed an interest in *stories* (more formally, *narratives*) for the way in which they function to provoke imagination—the formation of images, *icons*—that transform and deepen insight into and comprehension of oneself and one's world, and can also shape personal and communal identity in profoundly constructive and creative ways. This discovery has fueled my de-sire to explore the ways in and through which the use of *faithful-imagination* in biblical study and reflection enhances the process of spiritual comprehension and internalization of this vibrant and vital material—whether in narrative, poetic, prosaic, or didactic form. In the simplest of terms, the variegated faith traditions of both Jewish and Christian communities, while affirming the nec-essary cautions against an *overly* subjective, privatized, and self-serving interpretation of the biblical text(s), have also and at the same time advocated—in a variety of ways—that the imagination plays a key (if not *central*) role in comprehension of the deepest meaning(s) of Scripture and applicability to life. It has been my experience that to the degree I freely and in *good faith* open heart, mind, soul, and spirit to the guidance of the Spirit, allowing my imagination to be taken captive, new vistas of deeper and more penetrating insight and comprehension are realized.

The poems offered in the first chapter of this book are the *fruit* of such a reflective process of biblical study and reflection. I offer them as one model and one step in the whole program of biblical study for the purposes of preaching and teaching in the church. Of course I will have more to say about this in the *Introduction.* For the moment, I hope it is sufficient to say that what is offered in the first chapter, i.e. the biblical passages, poems, and etchings, coalesce to form a *family-portrait of grace and faith,* as I have come to live and share in the beauty and burdens of both with numerous Christian disciples, in a host of social and cultural settings, over the span of more than thirty years of ordained pastoral ministry.

When my brother—a professional artist—agreed to provide an artistically-crafted response to these poems, he had no way of knowing either the source of their inspiration in the respective biblical passages, nor the intention for which they had been written and collected. I simply sent Patrick copies of the poems requesting that he react—with pen and ink—to each in turn and as he felt led—or more accurately—*inspired.* The *fruit* of his employment of *faithful-imagination* is dramatically evident in his etchings. Patrick's etchings served to reinforce my own postulate that the Spirit operates to open and direct the imagination in a process of deepening insight and comprehension. The biblical passages, which initially generated and served as inspiration for the poems, and the poems that subsequently inspired the etchings, worked together in advancing a profound insight into the spiritual dynamics to be discovered in this practice of biblical reflection, while at the same time disclosing the *esthetics* of God's grace. In essence, each etching testifies to a comprehension of the biblical passage/paradigm that was not made available to Patrick and yet is thematically captured so graphically in the *spiritual fruit* of his artistic imagination!

I take this opportunity to thank the countless people who, over the years, have taken time and energy, care and devotion, in reading all of the poems collected here, while yet in manuscript form. Their constructive and helpful criticisms only improved my struggling efforts at clarity; I alone take credit for the residual inadequacies of the end product. More particularly, I thank my brother, Patrick, for the gift of his creative work and for his gracious contribution to this work.

And above all, I thank the God and Father of our Lord Jesus Christ who, in the power of the Holy Spirit has, time and again, been present to open my heart, mind, soul, and spirit—and yes, my *faithful-imagination* to the treasures of grace and faith. To God be the Glory!

Artist's Foreword

INSPIRATION FOR my brother's poems came with a rush. With pen in hand I read the first of twenty-three wonderful pieces, filled visually around prose and hope. I drew as though in a hypnotic state, thinking only long enough in some sort of pause, about the moments read—line after line—in human spiritual need lying before me.

Technically the drawings are pen and ink; no guidelines were given, nor did I feel any would be appropriate to what I wanted to convey. *Tormented Temple* was the first drawing; from that very moment *inspiration* began building. As pen scratched across paper, my mind followed my hand, following words, creating images so vivid that, at times, I could barely stop to take a breath. How totally wonderful!

After completing six etchings I shared them with a friend. Both poems and etchings so impressed and moved her, I thought: "This can only be the *inspiration* of God!" I called my brother the following day, telling him I was most impressed by his creation of inspirational, moving, lyrical—almost song-like—poems. I also explained that I was so moved by these poems, I could barely keep pen on paper—it seemed to float across the page as if guided by another hand.

Collaborating with Bert was a great joy for me. The verse and etchings work in a fluid, synthesized manner, creating a harmonic and insightful work of art.

I know our Creator would be proud!

Patrick Lee Walsh, Artist

Introduction

The New Testament has transformative power. There is nothing magical or even specifically theological in this: The reading of Shakespeare, after all, has created poets and lovers of poetry. What is specifically theological is the conviction of the church that this authoring power of the Scripture is activated by the Holy Spirit. All texts can transform, but these texts transform according to the mind of Christ

(1 COR. 2:16).[1]

THE INTENTION behind the observation of Luke Timothy Johnson differs from my own purpose; nevertheless, there are elements of his comment that can help in the attempt to articulate my own interest, e.g. his assertion of the way in which Scripture bears *transformative power* and *according to the mind of Christ*. These related observations contribute a theological content and clarity to my proposed approach to biblical reflection and meditation. Although Dr. Johnson restricts his comment to the New Testament, which is after all his primary focus, I have no doubt the same observation can be applied to the whole of the Bible—both Hebrew and Christian Scriptures. In this book I offer the end-product—what I prefer to call *fruit*—of a process of meditative-reflection on biblical passages, to demonstrate the viability of this approach as one thread in the overall tapestry of a more inclusive program of biblical study and reflection. I hope this offering discloses the way in which this particular practice of study and reflection contributes to an encounter with the *transformative power* of the biblical text. The proposed method of biblical engagement is

---

1. Johnson, *Scripture and Discernment*, 40.

not intended to circumvent the necessary and hard-work of historical, textual, and theological exploration; in fact, the method is enriched when one has taken the time to do the reading and research essential to fair and faithful exposition of any one biblical text.

Frankly, I am driven by two different, yet related, concerns: one is with the apparent lack of biblical and theological literacy and maturity in the church, and the second is with the way in which the artistic—or better said, *esthetic*—element has been underestimated for its value in making a contribution to an inclusive program of biblical reflection in the life of Western Christianity and devotional practices. I realize that both observations dabble in generalities, and yet would argue that even though they may appear *stereotypical*, they are no less valid! The contemporary church is clearly at risk, as generation-after-generation of *believers* fails to read and study the basic Text of the faith-community with any degree of sustained interest and prayerful intent. Biblical and theological illiteracy are at appalling levels in the current life of many if not most congregations and among Christians in general. I doubt that this is merely a "disease of mainline churches"—as I was recently told; even in the so-called "new paradigm" and "mega" churches, believers distance themselves from serious engagement with "the Book."

There are several consequences that arise from a lack of attention to and appreciation for the centrality of Scripture: an inability to clearly articulate the basic biblical doctrines of faith, difficulty in comprehending the symbolism of liturgy and life, lack of centeredness in addressing issues of grave importance to Christians, and an increase in individualism and subjectivism as the *primary* modes of decision making in the church, among others. However, no one concern has pressed itself upon my pastoral heart more than what I would call a *bankruptcy of Christian identity*, which I have undertaken to address in other publications. Here I will offer only some very general observations relevant to this proposed method of biblical engagement.

Acknowledging that my use of the term *Christian identity* could be read as a monosyllabic category—as in *one size fits all*—I contend that there are and have always been criteria by which one could identify Christian character as fundamental to personal identity.

Granted, identity is pliable and infused, shaped, and provided content through contextual realities, so that the Russian Orthodox Christian would have aspects of his/her Christian identity that would not *necessarily* be evident in that of—say—someone in either the Reformed or Lutheran confessions of the Protestant tradition. If, however, Luke Timothy Johnson's observation is viable, as I believe it to be, than one could suggest that a characteristic of *Christian identity* common to all believers and as a component of character formation, would be the *mind of Christ*—in all of the intricate and elaborate ways that biblical phrase can be construed. Yet it seems to me that this only begs the question: *What, in particular, are the essential elements evident in the "mind of Christ?"* Dr. Johnson answers that same question in some detail, with particular interest in those elements important to his purpose, which is discernment and decision making in the church.[2]

I would suggest that one element in defining the *mind of Christ* would be directly related to Jesus' use of *faithful-imagination* as a tool for disclosing God's grace, often concealed beneath and within the everyday realities of life and living. In other words, I believe that when Jesus uses parables and dramatic images he does so for the purposes of both disclosure (i.e. *revelation*) and mentoring in the faithful employment of human imagination, fostered in and guided by the Holy Spirit. Much of religious conviction and practice—both then and now—favor one of two extremes: either, too objective and cerebral (*abstract and propositional*) at the cost of heartfelt and esthetic, or too subjective and emotional (*senti-*

2. Ibid., 127–130.

mental and relative) at the cost of intellect and reason. Jesus' use of *faithful-imagination* is paradigmatic of the unity of heart and mind as a more holistic approach to expressing one's biblical and theological convictions as truth-claims. Demonstration of having the *mind of Christ* would not exclude the use of *faithful-imagination* in both the exploration and exposition of the Bible, and in giving expression to God's grace in the world through appropriate use of esthetics.

While Jesus may not have invented parables and the use of dramatic narrative or imagery in teaching, which was in evidence historically as a teaching method that preceded Jesus by at least hundreds of years, he made use of those same practices to enrich the use of *faithful-imagination* in unpacking spiritual dynamics; in so doing Jesus lent a degree of credibility to this process of study, reflection, and devotional practice. More importantly, the use of *faithful-imagination*—as a revelatory device—seems to suggest that recognition and reception of God's *revelation* itself requires a certain openness of heart, mind, soul, and spirit to the *esthetic* quality embedded in and characteristic of Holy Scripture and the imaginative process itself. The *mind of Christ* finds expression in both the individual Christian and the *household of God* through a faithful use of human imagination. This element of the *mind of Christ* is, therefore, one of the essential dimensions to what constitutes and characterizes Christian identity as *Christian*! It has been said that "the Christian life . . . is a richly symbolic life, offering us many windows into the mysteries beyond our commonplace lives. We (Christians) live truly when we live 'poetic lives.'"[3]

To the degree that Christian disciples are freed from the narrow constraints of an either too cerebral or too emotional expression of faith, and to the extent that they are encouraged to allow the imagination to come under captivity to the *mind of Christ*—i.e. to live "poetic lives"—they will also be liberated to read the Bible with alertness to the artistic-disclosure of God's grace throughout.

3. Houston, *The Heart's Desire*, 174.

In effect, encouraging the employment of *faithful-imagination* in the discipline of biblical study and reflection holds promise of fulfilling that which the Church catholic has always known to be true: the sheer magnitude of God's gracious *revelation* has demonstrated a multiplicity of esthetic-artistic expressions:

> Since all our keys are lost or broken,
> Shall it be thought absurd
> If for an art of words I turn
> Discreetly to the Word?
>
> Drawn inward by his love, we treasure
> Art to its secret springs:
> What, are we master in Israel
> And do not know these things?
>
> Lord Christ from out of his treasury
> Brings forth things new and old:
> We have those treasures in earthen vessels,
> In parables he told.
>
> And in the single images,
> Of seed, and fish, and stone,
> Or shaped in deed and miracle,
> To living poems grown.[4]

In this offering I am, essentially, pleading with the church—in her various confessions and configurations—to rekindle within the community of believers a free exploration of the richness of the biblical text, with special attention to the employment and maturation of the *faithful-imagination* in reading, study, reflection, meditation, and exposition; this itself is an act of faith in seeking to mature in one aspect of what it means to have the *mind of Christ*.

4. Ibid.

I am of the conviction that such practice—should it take hold and root within the Christian community—would serve to strengthen the *transformative* process through which the church can experience the vitality and reality of the *mind of Christ* and further maturation of an identity that is uniquely *Christian* in orientations and expression of belief.

While I am not providing a detailed description of the approach and assessment of its possibility for further development as devotional practice, I am hopeful that in sharing the *fruit* of my own use of this more *esthetic* method of biblical reflection, other Christians will be encouraged to return to the exploration of their primary Text, with renewed desire to engage its profound depth and in openness to the Holy Spirit, who guides an awakening to the *esthetic-artistic*—and therefore the *beautiful*—characteristic of Scripture as a whole. The poems and portraits collected in this book are humbly offered as evidence of the intrinsic power of the proposed methodology. There is no way to give full expression to the issues of transformation and identity, except to say that both my brother and I have testified on numerous occasions to the way in and through which the employment of this method of biblical reflection deepened our appreciation for the *rich texture of revelatory encounter* and greater comprehension of the profuse and *esthetic-disclosure of God's grace* in the world—both within and around us. There has been a remarkable *transformation* in the way we have come to understand ourselves and our world in relation to the God who *etches* and *poetically-words* his grace into both creature and creation.

Whether the reader is a lay person, working in disciplined fashion to open Scripture to others in his/her community of faith, or the pastor bent over his/her desk in the faithful effort to unpack another deep, and perhaps laborious, passage of Scripture, I pray that the proffered *fruit* of this proposed method of biblical reflection will ignite a spark of new insight and Spirit-driven creativity. I pray that you, too, will discover how the Spirit awakens the imaginative process, and in doing so offers refreshing insights, transformative power, and the promise of growth and enrichment as we seek to live in and express ourselves through the *mind of Christ.* Beyond that I pray that interest in the proposed method of biblical reflection and the *fruit* offered make possible a renewed appreciation in the Church catholic for the revelatory power of the esthetic-artistic—whether visual or literary. And I cannot help but wonder if this awakening to the process of *faithful-imagination* will not also bring about a deeper appreciation for that *transcendental characteristic* of God, which seems to have been lost on far too many believers in Western Christianity—that is, *Beauty*!

PART ONE

The Drama of God's Grace
in Poem & Portrait

THE FOLLOWING poems were born in the process of reflection on select passages of Scripture. The poems were forwarded to my brother and he graciously provided the images associated with each of the poems offered. My brother, Patrick's, only expressed wish was that each of the etchings follow immediately the poem that inspired the image; in this way he hoped that the reader would take time for reflection as he or she spent time with each poem and its corresponding etching.

THE BEGINNING

(Based on: Genesis 1:1–2; John 1:1–3; Mark1:1)

"In the beginning . . ."
A home hammered-out of dream, longing, hope;
hard wood and nails formed from hearts held together by
love and care.
"In the beginning . . ."
A lifetime of travel; crawl, step, strut, stumble,
fall, flat; age comes slowly, first lines seen, soon
grow old; sleep, sleep long and low in earth's womb.
"In the beginning . . ."
A faith forged on the hard steel of some other's witness;
the slow growth, moving into the morning of memory;
awakening to a sweet song; come to life, to live, to die;

the start, the end, the last-to-first—
daybreak.
"In the beginning . . ."
A message crossing over, from above; a message to take
captive, and break chains; a message drifting on some
gentle breeze of wings and wonder; a message to
make, break, cut, cure, end, open, close—
create.
"In the beginning . . ."
A Word to walk across the waters of our tempestuous
hearts.
A Word wet, to wash the stain and soothe, cool;
feel it over heated longing.
A Word, breath and soft whisper, drawing our
scorched souls deep,
deeper into a dark mystery.
A Word held out in calloused hands—hard and holy.
A Word there, here, at some far,
far horizon.
A Word waiting to be told, touched, tasted.
"In the beginning . . ."

WASHED

(Based on: Exodus 14:21–22; Mark 1:4–5;
Romans 6:1–4)

Turn, take off your skin of soulful loss;
down, down beneath the dark wet, wild flow,
over the rounded shoulders, rolled back—hair
hanging with drip, eyes now wide before the final
burial—beneath the watery grave—thrice bowed.
Life looks distorted from the watery place of new
birth; voices above, muffled into senseless sound;
only the heart-beat breaks the silence within, and
the mind races over the rough terrain of memory.
Now up; lifted out, over, above, forever
Freed.
Death has touched this frail-frame; below that current
of confession a Spirit is felt—holding, hearing;
a surgical slice into changed life at the heart.
Sky, sun, clouds, birds, trees, friends, strangers;
all witness this wonder of the water's womb giving
birth to a new child,
with holy benediction.

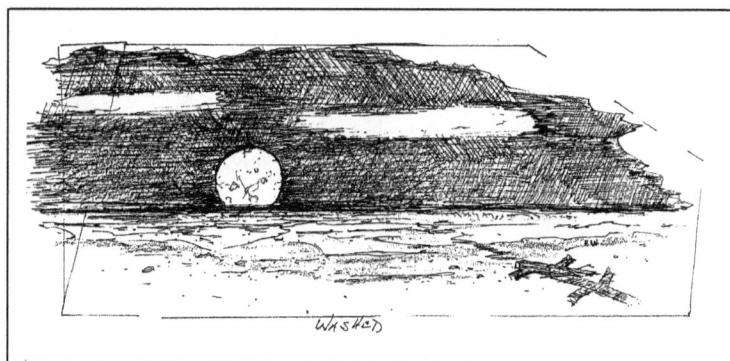

WASHED

THE VOICE OF ONE CRYING

(Based on: Psalm 40:1–3; Mark 1:2–3; Romans 8:15–17)

Bent back against a gnarled tree, older than life;
holding the fading flower, with large eyes in framed face,
famine in human form; small, tender, with death in lips
parched; that mother-mourning;
"the voice of one crying . . . ."
Locked door, hammered by the heart wanting in—
tossed away, this life with a river-line of need running up
her arm;
pleads for passion, with parent beyond the wooden wall, tears,
trembling; that was once my child—lost
long, long way back—lost
to broken trust—thrust a spike with poison into her
arm, heart, soul—crouching at her door;
"the voice of one crying . . . ."
Wires, wound, soft sound of breathing toward end,
corner darkened by shadow; small life on large white
    landscape of
lifelessness; one, two, three,
watch and wait and wonder when the call will come—when?
Tears and often,
"the voice of one crying . . . ."
Wild eyes, flashing faith; hold on to every word he
cries-out;
this camel-haired-prophet, spewing salvation's sweet nectar,
promising the coming of
Compassion, and
Healing in heaven-scent wines;
listen, listen, listen—
"the voice of one crying . . . ."

The Voice of one Crying

TORMENTED TEMPLE

(Based on: Psalm 69:1–3; Mark 1:23–24; Romans 8:18–21)

They call me the aborted child of darkness;
my soul, they say, is soured from the breath of demons.
Never one with whom to play, climb that corner tree,
toss pebbles at old women bent low at the well.
Never held in arms of comfort, drenched in care or
tender eyes, touched by the soft hand of compassion.
Never the stare of desire, the kiss of honeyed lips, the whisper
of longing fulfilled.
Never, never—for me.
My synagogue is there on the street called "Despair,"
where I sit, bound in a corner, untouched by the Lord's
love.
"Quiet!" My prayers, mumbled through twisted lips;
each word forced from my darkness to that distant light of
longing.
"Quiet!"
I hope and cry and die, hope and cry and die—weep
a thousand deaths each day.
Come, O come, come and free these captive bones,
this twisted flesh, this demented soul.
I want to sing, to see, to stand—while—
Lord, come to this dark corner; it's only my life—
But it's life, Lord. Am I
Your own?
Bent low beneath hard rain; cold, comfortless, waiting.

Tormented
Temple

VOICED VICTORY

(Based on: Psalm 22:1–2, 12a–14; Mark 1:25–26; Romans 8:27–30)

We cannot abandon the only home we have ever known,
only to haunt the hollow spaces of time lost;
this human soul is our possession-possessed at its creation.
The reason for the sale of soul to slavery, long, long
passed into the shadows of yesterday; still heard in their question:
"Who sinned . . . ?"
They foolishly think they see so clearly; so simple to post the
fault, to hang it all on the peg of something called
"sin."
The dark night of our triumphal cry, now
silenced by the voice of this silly carpenter;
calling like a farmer to his swine: "Come out! Come out!"
We will not turn away from loyalty to the one who
is instigator of all evil, gives lust, feeds our ravenous desires.
We will not relent of this human space, our
combat, our last ditch; call, and call, and call again, never
will we become your captives—carpenter!
What power, rope, chain, claim pulls us from this house of
human flesh?
What voice comes like water, raging, washing us away, away?
Cry, scream, cling; our hold, lost—falling into empty—our being
blasted; our strength now weakness; our loss his gain.
Outside, no longer safe, we see him who was our refuge,
    our toy—
taken into the arms of Another.

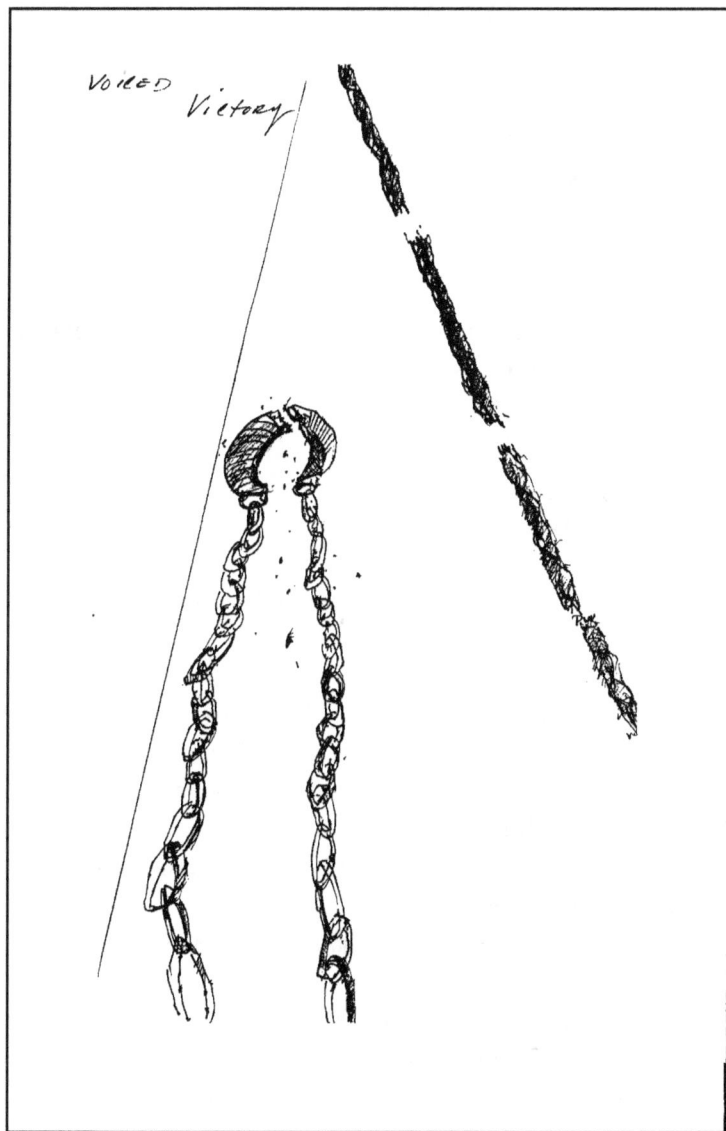

VOILED *Victory*

LONGING'S LOOK

(Based on: Psalm 70:1–3a, 4b-5; Mark 1:21–28;
Galatians 5:24–25)

Another service of song and prayer played-out on the stage of
this old synagogue.
Years and years of prayer and praise and spoken promises,
to which we've all tied our dreams—believing
as we must in the mercy greater than old Job's tortured frame,
huddled there in his own corner.
I've wondered what brings old Job to this place where
holy people hold him suspect,
at arms length;
some in sacred-hate for the sin that sold his soul to such
captivity.
I've often wondered why his lips mumble prayers
    to a Lord looking
the other way;
wondered why he doesn't hang himself from the corner tree;
wondered what meaning faith has when borne by such misery.
Old Job rocks and rolls, back and forth to the rhythm
    of the Rabbi's
voice, to scriptural song; something like a smile breaks his
broken face—and mine.
Somewhere in my soul, a rumble, like a stomach calling
    for food—
a beginning of a plea for old Job forming
at my throat, held for a moment—and then
"Come, O comforting One, come to free old Job—
Come and give him—us—life!"
Old Job turns from his far corner—locks his face on mine,
looking, longing for mercy.
Aren't we all?

DANGEROUS DREAM

(Based on: Genesis 28:10–12; Mark 2:8–11; 1 Corinthians 13:13)

Last night a dream; it was last night—a dream
crept upon me like fog, morning mist drifting over the lake,
soft, slow, shapeless—something.
A dream, I'm sure it was a dream of shadowy figures
and faces I know, save one—strange.
"Dreams" my dear-dead-mother would say to her wrecked-child,
"dreams, my son, simply drop-down from heaven."
This dream; I try to shake it from my soul; despite
    my mother's
words—dreams are dangerous.
I have gone to that world many, many nights and
days; tormented by dreams of dearer life; to dance my way to
festival; drop to my knees in prayer; toss the nets and retrieve
them with strong arms.
To dream, to die; dreams are dangerous.
Last night, a dream took shape within my memory;

a dream, last night, that I cannot escape. And the sound of
His voice
shatters my faithless soul:
"Rise, take your pallet, and go!"

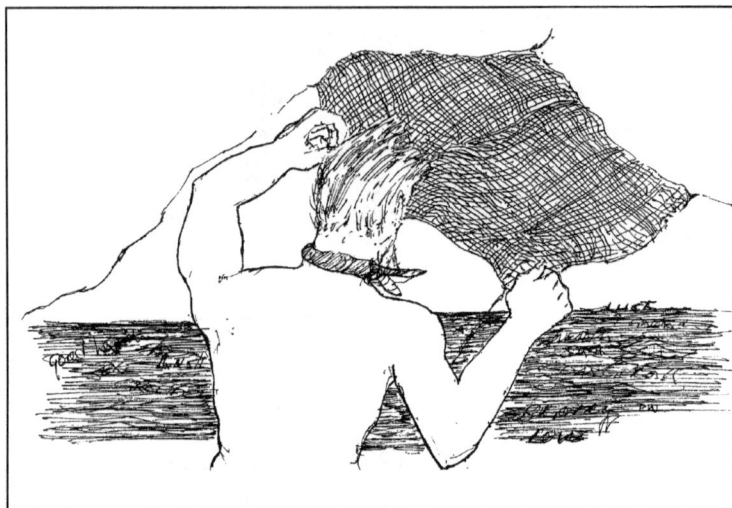

FAITH'S FORM

(Based on: Genesis 12:1–3; Mark 2:1–5; Hebrews 11:1–2)

I remember sitting at the Rabbi's feet,
listening to stories of faith; some fearless warrior
strong to fight the Lord's cause;
some stammering shepherd, a renegade-prince,
redeemer of my people; some girl
risking life and limb to save strangers for a Savior's worship,
    his own.
Faith on faith took shape on storied lips; and I remember
faith; not
blind obedience, but the strength to be for other's cause, a
claim to promise.
I remember as I feel my grip, my leathered hand holding

its own place—while three friends hold theirs as well—and
this:
a batch of twisted branches, covered with flesh, smelling of
death—a mother's motionless nightmare.
"Early or late," cries Nathan, "we'll remove the roof-top
if we must!
We'll drop him down on people's heads, if we must!"
I wonder:
What must it be to have a brother all-broken and twisted,
like this?
It must be faith straining at my arms and legs,
bearing this mat,
misery dripping over its edges;
faith,
bearing sin and sickness to the Story-teller with
Saving touch.

WORDED WONDER

(Based on: Deuteronomy 26:1–2, 5–9;
Mark 2:12; Galatians 1:3–5)

Long, long I have walked these dusty streets,
all along the way dropping words down peoples ears;
hope against hope that someone—if not some—will hear.
Words and words and Word—all with a power to cleanse and
claim their hearts, again;
walking village to village with hope that someone will hear,
hold, heal.
And here I Am again, looking into the faces, a countless mass of
known-unknowns—known to One, so well their hairs
    are counted—
each—all.
Faces with the stain of life clinging to them all, each and all;
wanting,
not words, but a blast of heaven's own breath—the sacred staff
of Moses, lifted high above their embattled hearts to bring
    victory, or
to part their troubled waters to salvation.
Perhaps Elijah's bath to wash the leper's stain from their
souls.
Surrounded by the sights and sounds of human hunger, thirst,
lacerated spirits;
heaven above, suddenly visible—I remember their
eyes—longing.
The sudden sound of anguished release as another frame of
twisted muscle and bone begins to move for the first time;
and glory breaks-out all over.
I hear His voice: "My Son, I saw you long ago when woven in
your mother's womb—you were, as you are—Mine.
I've waited with long, silent, pain for your return to Me—

My Word—
My Wonder—
My Worded-Wonder."

GRINDING OF TEETH

(Based on: 2 Kings 19:11–13; Matthew 22:1–14;
Hebrews 12:25a)

The long, hard distance between my now and then
cannot ease the desperate longing in this eternal
night of impassioned plea.
Sitting, eyes strained and stained by tormented tears;
my inner self turns sour in the memory of sinful
fear, while the "faithful" look-on from a far away lighted
love.
The sound can cut its way into the very core of your soul;
more, more, so much more torturous than was the lament of
women-wailers.
This cry, with stone-on-stone shiver, sets teeth on edge and tells
of the price paid for fear.

Would that we could turn this world around and make our
    way back
to those choices—seen so clearly in their
consequence.
Would that our graceless grinding of teeth could reach Him
    who once
held such trust in our own heart's love and loyalty.
Would that He would even "still, small voice" that Word
    to liberate
our longing for relief.
But now—another sound echoes down the emptied corridors
    of my soul,
and I sink:
"Throw him into the outer darkness!"

A COMMUNAL CRY FOR MERCY
(Based on: Psalm 20:1–4; Luke 13:6–9; Philippians 2:3–5)

We who were once His friends pray the Master will
relent,
repent of that ruin and rejection inflicted on infidelity.
We who were once His friends look upon this
judgment,
and wonder if we too might one day having faith in faith,
face that same final word of exclusion.
We who once sat at table with this fallen Friend hope that
the Master's well-known
mercy,
will heal the broken spirit of this fragile world.
We who once knew communion, laughter, tears, joy, and
shared service now see ourselves in him who
failed through fear;
our love for him has not been lost as we long for
redemption.
We who sin and suffer temptation, touch that all-too-human
heart,
confess that we might one day disappoint our Master's
entrusted coinage, and
condemnation
weigh-down our weary souls.
We who found His judgment harsh, now come to Him
    each day,
and for our fearful, foolish friend, cry-out:
"Mercy, Master! Have mercy!"

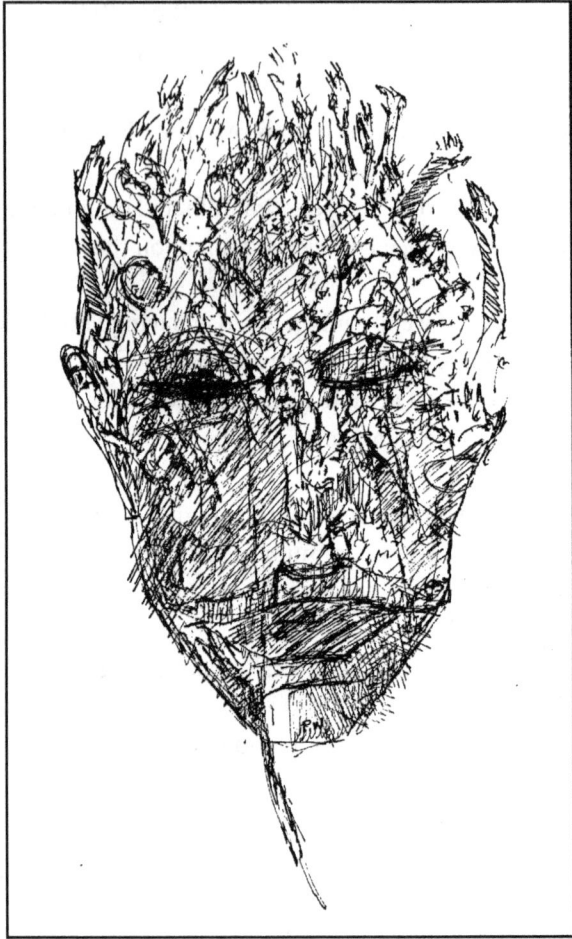

GUARDIAN ANGEL

(Based on: Psalm 91:9–12; Matthew 18:10; Hebrews 1:14)

With sharp winged shoulder, there—unseen sentinel;
keeper of soul; eyes radiant and fixed—finding,
exploring, probing, commanding as commanded.
Sweet scent of sacred smoke clings to this guardian's
bright-white; brilliant, blinding obedience to One—this soul is
safe and saved.

ROAD KILL

(Based on: Psalm 8:6–7; Matthew 6:26a; Revelation 21:1, 5a)

We are not blind to the death, dark against the heated tar;
Small, now with bent paws, deformed in a form of
prayer;
foreign to those pious passengers—passing;
passing along, around death's victim, now gazing at the sky with
vacant eyes.
Yet I do wonder what coldness has so gripped our souls,
that these tortured frames merely amuse or annoy us.
They are no less life from Divine Delight than is
that beloved bundle beneath the blanket of
cardboard on the grate.
When next you fly-by—pause in prayer;
May God forgive this mercilessness—for it seeps into
the human heart and will not allow compassion for
Christ's children.

PARISHIONER'S PLEA

(Based on: Isaiah 44:6–8; John 1:14; 1 Corinthians 2:1–5)

Pass along some word; a word clothed in something more than
jeans and sweat-shirt; a word to
wrap around these tired, tortured bones.
Speak;
and in speaking pour out oil and wine, rich—and
break-bread with your lips;
for these live long—and longer still
their hunger.
Speak;
and pass along a word with a human heart, a beat in
Highest Heaven's breast.

IN MEMORIAM

(Based on: Isaiah 42: 15–16; Luke 4:18–19;
2 Corinthians 4:16–18)

Today that sighted-soul, with eyes long closed to this world,
beheld that Glory beyond the sun's blinding glare.
She whose darkened sight could not—never—prevent her
vision of a Father's faith-unseen within.
For a moment, my heart held its breath, mindful
that this fleshy emblem of a Divine mercy had taken leave of
mortal life.
To life she now wings her way, and from Abraham's heart
   beholds
with healed sight, her
Savior.

WINGED GRACE

(Based on: Matthew 6:25–26)

Sparrow, small; grace given wing; suffer not to fall,
hard; God is
watching.
A watchful eye keeps pressed against your tiny frame in
flight;
some Carpenter with splintered hands has lifted a
Holy word to hold your small life in
timeless honor.

SCRIBAL WITNESS

(Based on: Deuteronomy 10:12–16;
Mark 2:5–11; Galatians 3:5–7)

To testify to what I've seen, or, to take you
back to that blasphemy is more than my Torah-soul
can take.
My Father passed down to me the task of keeping faith
free; on his dying bed I pledged my heart and soul to
serve the Law of Moses—with tears, bind myself to
keep pure that precious gift of our gracious Lord.
Then—to hear this wandering rabbi speak such
scandal, in the presence of all gullible hearts and
minds, had me
furious.
Foundations of heaven, shaken by this silly fool who
dares to claim Divine right—or—
so I thought, I think; I don't know.
That poor twisted soul shook-off his paralysis, like a
dog shaking-off water; freed—
he took time to stand, arms out-stretched to heaven—as if to
offer praise.
Some day when the Lord allows me to question at His feet,
I'll ask in faith:
"How, dear Lord, how is it that the crippled could walk,
    and yet—
the sighted—
not see?"
For now? I've committed myself to keep Torah and—
faith.

PARABLE OF PAIN

(Based on: Psalm 77:1–4; Luke 12:16–21;
1 Corinthians 10:12–13)

Every day, in this darkness, where shadows
move, casting ghost-like images before my eyes,
I remember the ruinous judgment that cast my soul
down into this dark abyss.
A world apart from the world; that warm and lighted
world in which love and laughter create and revive
life abundant;
A world that was once home, where I held hope and delighted in
dreaming.
Yet here, now, my heart has been abandoned to
any and every dread; I am forever entangled in this
strong web of fear; I cannot hear the
human voice; cut-off from
freedom's embrace.
Is it forever?
My memories have become monsters; demons have tormented,
     and keep
alive the pain of this well-planned punishment.
Memories of those moments in time when my Master trusted
me;
placing in my feeble hands the wealth of His world.
Memory presses for a mercy larger than
life itself.
Blackness is pierced by a far, far distant light;
and my straining eyes look for that light to drain the
darkness of the darkest hour, drawing my soul to deliverance.
The parable of pain is my life; and the long, long
Love of God is that final Word on all wasted
"talents."
God's grace is ever greater than any failure of
faith.

SO I WAS AFRAID

(Based on: Exodus 3:11–12; Luke 19:11–27; Acts 5:1–6)

It once came as a knotted rope in my gut; as
father stood above me—a towering reproach—with
more than mere displeasure in his dark eyes.
The soft light of his parental-love, extinguished; and now,
a look that called and cut my soul.
A whirlwind blew about my head, as his words,
heated by a wounded heart, beat against and
seared my conscience.
It once came as the taunting claim from the trusted mouth of
a best friend;
the dare to drop myself from on high.

My youthful bones cried-out for caution, and warned of
what pain could follow my following this friend's folly.
And with one great sigh I turned
back—and broke the bond between us.
It once came in the fair-face of another, who stood
apart and claimed my affections; yet—
it laid a greater claim to my commitment, drawing me from
her voice, into
a very dark and lonely space.
Now I watch, with tormented remembrance, as she
goes on.
It once came as the time to cast myself into a noble
cause; the cries of other stricken-souls bid me
touch, take in hand, bind, bind the broken flesh and bone.
Yet it whispered that such a task could be my last—and
for the lost—I'd lose myself.
It once came as my Master's trust with hand-held-treasure to
make grow; while other voices urged caution, catching-up my
heart.
I listened, life-long, to that dark and desperate whisper,
    giving-over
my world to fear.
A deepening darkness has claimed me as its own.

THE FISHERMAN

(Based on: Isaiah 6:1, 5–8; Matthew 4:18–20;
Acts 2:41–42)

Old, bent, face of flint; eyes bent hard against
blinding sun,
radiant reflection in crystal blue;
his hope takes form as a line draped out over
water;
with smoke flowing from his face; a mimic of
Mt. Sinai;
a tiny-god to this realm of water.
And hidden beneath that looking glass are
scaled warriors; fully unaware, yet—
ready to take his offering.

LABORED LOVE

(Based on: Genesis:33:1–4; Luke 6:35–36;
1 Corinthians 13:4–7)

Long the pain placed between them; hard spike, driven
deep into a Delicate soul;
Words to wound, without intention,
bleed nonetheless.
Children, take care with what calls your heart its home.
Parents, say that which is a sacred Word,
entrusted to your care;
"My child, my joy, my heart!"
I have witnessed this wonder of redemption—three spikes
driven into the heart of God's most Precious—and a
loyal, labored love is
its marker.

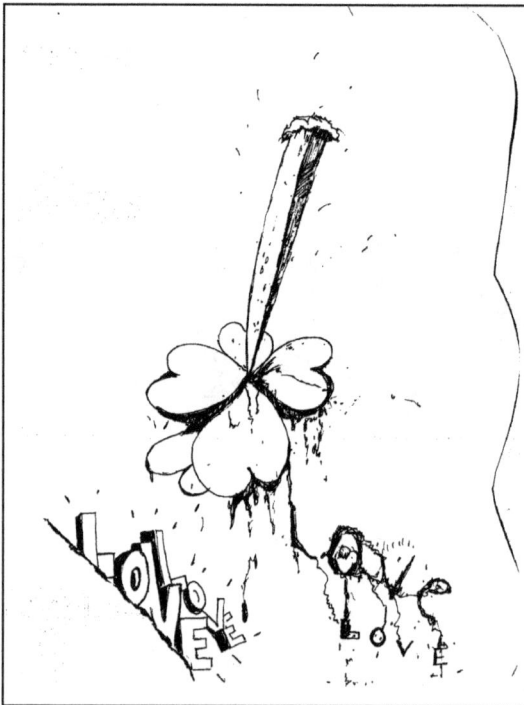

WITH BROKEN BEAUTY

(Based on: Hosea 2:14–15; Matthew 23:37–39; 2 Corinthians 5:18–21)

Wave upon wave, rise and fall and rise again;
her gentle form to meet me, and greet me with
gracious invitation—City of God—Holy Hill!
To enter her world, to gift and be given Love's greatest
Glory.
Her eyes are deep in hidden heartache; held as they are held
firm against betrayal; broken, broken by—
human indifference; and all have in turn
violated that most sacred trust.
God gave her heart,
love—held out to such who saw—yet,
cared only for self, and sank
their blood-thirsty greed into her gentleness—to—
gulp.
Time and tender Truth will heal her wound, as God
gives again a Love—too long to
measure—Holy Hill—City of God!

LONGING

(Based on: Genesis 6:5–8; Matthew 13:16–17; 2 Timothy 4:6–8)

In the silence within I find, again, with
eyes of gentle invitation,
deep and mysterious,
Your Love rises above and with softness,
embraces.
What of this waiting world, this incessant
longing, this unrelenting
desire?
It will burn, fire, white-hot, to purge my
heart for Him.
Look then, now, your soft Spirit sweeps my
face, fragrant.
Look, now, my arms enfold an
Eternal Joy.
I am short on patience and long on
longing to see and hear—Christ, when?
All longing lasts, but lasts only for a time.
Promises of His coming come and go—longing
lasts, as long as there is time.
Time is fleeting as His heart leads us Home.

Part Two

Poems: Slices of Life

THE POEMS collected in this chapter were written over a period of twenty years; some represent reflections on the spiritual dynamics of life, while others are more romantic in nature. All have their origins in both the genuine realities of life, and several derive from the joy and pain of pastoral experience. It is my conviction that poetry provides us with an alternative lens for looking through at our world; a world in which so much appears—and perhaps is—little more than mundane. Even so, as stated by way of the hymn verse in the dedication, *(God) shines in all that's fair;* faith is—at least—the capacity to see with new eyes this world of God's creating and sustaining providence and love. I am admittedly a novice in this fine art of poetic expression, but have in this collection, no less than in the previous chapter's poems, listened attentively to a guiding and creative voice (whom I would call "Holy Spirit"), in the desire to be both faithful and honest in the following expressions of life—*slices of life.*

GRIEF

Touched beneath tearful willow; sky
concealed by soft green, peaking
blue and sun gold all over her.
How lost I am to look at her, in her;
feeling my heart, or her own, as a
rhythm of passion and grace;
pouring out and drenching with sorrow's salty sea.
Touched by her tears on my cloth;
joy now awaits another day, and
fulfillment of a dream—
long in waiting, waking;
I smile to soften the darkness of nights,
yet in my soul a sadness burns
with the glow of dying embers.
I cannot breathe—I will not breathe—
This is all of it.

FOR AN UNKNOWN LOVE

Come softly to her and take what time
will allow for watching her sleep—
soft in the night of her dreaming.
Lean slowly and sing a melody of
compassion for the care and laughter
she brings
to your wounded heart and bruised soul.
Lift her hair from almond eyes—press one
kiss to her lips,
trace the contours of her cheek with gentle
and courteous hand.
Wait—wait—for her sigh, the whisper of
love, the warm glow of love will burn brighter.
This night I give her my heart, again;

and she is the love my soul breathes in—
and she is the devotion my heart craves—
and she is the tender truth of every today
and all tomorrows.

THERE IS A SONG

There is a Song that fills my soul,
at night, in dark and then at dawn;
a Song with melody unrehearsed, and
every note comes with touch of grace.
The lyric is His opus, a Word of
inexpressible Joy composed
in Love.
The Word melts into the soul, beneath
the warmth of Passion's breathless sigh;
where His heart whispers to my waiting heart.
And the Song is His gracious Gospel.

SOFT ON THE AIR

Soft on the air, gentle comes the sweet
fragrance of His love;
lavished on the wounded heart of one
who yearns, longs for night to give to
night an eternal embrace.
My gracious Lord whose tender touch is
Love;
Love that binds two hearts—above—below—in the eternal
Ecstasy of two made one in Him.

ADAM'S MEMORY

A day of silent snow, falling from a gray sky;
my heart held in a mild smile, a bright laugh,

a loving gaze, a voice of unfamiliar cords.
The water itself, breaking over rocks and
fallen stumps—it sings;
the water gave itself to that same song, there to
serenade such beauty as rested sweetly on my mind.
I watched her move, her face radiant with charm.
I watched her give herself to dreams of delight, to be
then—not now.
I watched her soft form, held against leafless trees,
her every step a sight to behold; and in the wonder—
took her into my soul.
My memory of that one day brings light, like
a candle glowing in the frost-burdened window of
a cottage in winter.
All warmth is in the light of her.

ANOTHER STARLESS NIGHT: PETER THE APOSTLE

And in the velvet blackness of another starless night,
I linger on my thoughts of Him, having nothing to hold but
Hope.
This is such a strange, bewildering love; to gaze once again into
those eyes so far, so near—to feel my heart heaving in
    my chest
with the excitement of each new word He spoke.
Today I could not even touch the memory of His voice,
    while in that
very hour I yearned for just a word.
The murmur of human need crept in and there I was—
covered by a command I will never escape!
How much I wanted to be with Him, yet separate again.
Faithful to follow Him who calls through human cares;
One drenched in the delight of serving others.
Yet I am not so blessed.

And so I see hour-by-hour slip away, and that weighted silence
wears on my soul.
Sing Sweet Bird! Sing—somewhere, anywhere!
Sing, even if only beneath your breath, and I swear
   I will hear
each note, each tender Word.
A thousand tomorrows stretch before my sight; looking to me
like connected memories of what might have been; if only
His hand should be in this, as in all; He must have purpose.
Someone—a Greek or a Prophet?—once said,
"Don't take love literally; take it lyrically!"
And if so, God must be the Supreme Poet to have penned the
Prose Christ is—in swaddling cloth, shadowed by a cross.
Such heavenly beauty balanced on His brow, fair, adorned with
unmeasured affection.
My memories on this starless night are but musings—or—
echoes from the bottom most confines of my heart and soul.
If I cannot see Him—if I must suspend all such delight
   for some
higher, more urgent cause;
then let these musings work harder still to tell of Him—
Dear Heart so wounded in the long road of Love.

SO, WHEN AT LAST I SPEAK

There is a love so deep and wide its Truth is beyond words;
and this causes my heart its deepest sorrow, because
   I cannot say
what I want most to have them hear; words to wash them
   in joy.
My soul stammers to speak the Beauty with which He has
   graced me.
I walk these feeble words through a thousand trials, hoping
   to purge them

of their human dross—weighted as they are to the world.
Yet when at last I speak them to their hearts, grace will touch
     their hidden
places; they in turn will touch His hem—and—new life unfold!
Night and shadows drift before my tired eyes, and under the
     watchful eye
of a million stars, I wonder—
where they are—
what they dream—
for what I want most is their delight in life and in Life.
So I whisper a prayer with words to reach-out and to enfold
     His heart and
claim His comfort, His courage, His constancy.
All my life long I have waited and now—
I look the fool; fumble for words, wanting to tell them what
     Joy awaits them in
His presence, His peace, His gracious smile.
Perhaps He will pardon this woeful messenger whose heart
     belongs to Him.

FOR THE HEART OF MY BELOVED

That balmy spring evening, a full moon suspended in a
     blue-gray sky;
I witnessed her soft-white light drench trees and robins.
There to sweetly serenade my beloved, as Solomon of old;
she on whom the moon's milky gaze had fallen, ever so softly
     disclosing
the sparkle of her voice.
With early evening stars peeking from behind angel-hair
     clouds,
I hold out my hand and tenderly receive hers—a gift.
Tremble to touch this delicate flesh, holding her hand
     in fascination

that she should welcome me to walk in her love.
Some voice from far away sings a melody, and I want
    to capture its
grace as a gift to my beloved.
It is more than I can bear to sit beside this creature who seems
    to me the
embodiment of elegance.
And as the night washes over her cheek, I glory in the moment.
There I reach a hand to brush back a lock of hair—hoping to
make her smile; sweet, soft, long.
What I cannot tell her is the wealth of affection I have in my
    heart;
and in this radiant night I pray for endless days to try—
    to try to speak
my love, my longing, my joy.
Tenderly I lean into the light of the moon on her cheek
    and speak
a word—while watching the stars take shape in her eyes.

SOME GLORIOUS DAY

Today I sat in silence and wondered what could be if
after this hard and troubling day I would come to lay my head
at His breast, and wear His warm embrace like a wool blanket
on a bitter winter's morning.
I set out to see this and that hungry soul;
hospitals, houses, tears and trembling hearts; to each I offer
a Word to heal the wound.
Yet all the while I feel my heart—drained of mercy—being
replenished by a Father's Love.
Always there, His soft touch taking the stain of sorrow from
my soul.
Always there, His nail-print-hands washing the worrisome
    thoughts

from my mind.
Always there, His gentle voice speaking words which fall softly
all over the struggles I feel—soothing, soothing.
Then I set out for home—and with Him;
His gentleness now draped over my discouraged, dispirited life.
I remember—*anamnesis*—I remember where my world is—
There in His heart; there in His love; there in His life—my
Eternal Home.
Slowly I sink back into what is this day—this day
   when I—where
I and He (Who is all grace!)—must wait in painful-pleasure.
As I turn from myself once again, headed for the front door of
another hospital, I stretch-out my hand—and for one brief, one
startling moment—I'm certain I feel the print of a nail.
Some day—some glorious Day—take thought—take heart—
take hope.

TOUCH THIS FRAGILE FLOWER

The first light of a new day drifts in
only to break, gently, across her waiting face;
and I awake to watch that striking transformation,
with the warm colors of summer bringing her gracious
features to fruition.
This moment, with the world still shrouded in sleep's silence,
calls my heart into her reverent pose.
One sudden sound, one unwanted motion would make for the
death of this delight.
Somewhere in her imagination she is greeted by joy, as
the witness forms on her tender lips—a smile, broad.
To awaken her would somehow be an act of sacrilege.
Rather, let me temper my trembling heart; let me instead
breathe each breath with her own; let me be warmed in the
light of her unspoken love for all things

living.
I will hold secret what I have seen; I will wait until another
Morning—and then—
Touch this fragile flower.

FOR ALL GOD'S PEOPLE (FOR HEIDELBERG)

If words could work a miracle, bring perpetual-pleasure to a
    Life-Lived;
I would rejoice to speak a thousand verbs and verses
    to enfold them
in His wonder, love, health and hope—
boundless all.
If dreams could work a miracle, bear the fulfillment
    of every yearning,
every longing and deep desire in a Life-Lived;
I would rejoice to imagine a thousand worlds in which
    their hearts would
overflow with eternal-pleasures.
If songs could work a miracle, sing the sweetest lyric
    to lift the soul
and lavishly lace a Life-Lived with graceful harmony;
I would rejoice to compose a thousand melodies
    to soothe their souls
with music—to bless them with a ballad of unending
    Affection.
If art could work a miracle, framing the world in colors
    resplendent,
golds and grays, crimson and blue, made to move the heart
    of a Life-Lived,
I would rejoice to take brush in hand, to take the pallet
    of a thousand
brilliant hues, to create a paradise of heavenly pleasures,
to paint their world a place of pure delight.

And if there is a miracle-made, it would be in this
    One-Life-Loved.
He—the Word, the Song, the Art; He the point of pleasure
    unparalleled;
He the fulfillment of time toward eternity;
He the treasure taken from the realm of heaven above
    and dropped as
the dew of a New Day into
the world
they know and love
reluctantly.

IN PARADISE

A summer moon crowds the canopy above, dropping white
    light over them.
The warm breath of God comes as a whisper; words of a song
    that is theirs
alone.
In the shadows, angels dance for joy; tree leaves applaud
    in praise.
Lyrics of love drip from the graceful pens of other heavenly
    heralds;
while the concealed witnesses of summer's night shield their
    eyes in reverent
embarrassment—and even hold their breath, stunned
    by such beauty.
What they share is a song, a gentle melody authored by that
    Mystery who speaks
down the corridors of centuries—"and the two shall become"—
    "and the two shall
become."
In this tepid wonderland, washed in the light
    of jubilant moon, he and she find

Life; they wait for Love's fruit to ripen, sweet.
She sits still, silent, in beauty unmatched.
Yet in her heart, a voice; playfully it discloses secret dreams,
    locked away for long
centuries.
He, like the trembling voyager enters into her eyes,
    beneath and below;
and there he discovers himself to be found by something
    Sacred.
All around her he witnesses furrowed wings; angels gather
    to bow before such
Grace.
The stars mill about while he and she sit side-by-side,
    within and without,
touching and untouched, tender and terrible in what
    they know.
Here two hearts have merged, submerged in the common
    soul that sours above and
beyond—words cannot wash away His powerful presence.
Somehow in the breath they breathe, a prayer ascends;
    warm and kind and complete.
Without a word, just one short sigh, and suddenly they are
    held by a Heart, breathing-out
a Rhythm of Passion, Promise:
"And the two shall become *one*."

POST-PARADISE

My restless heart wanders in a world without You.
Are You? Are You there or here?
Here, I wait, lonely and longing to lose myself in You
    once again.
Hoping—soon—to stand in that soft glow of Your radiance.
It is a moment of fascination and treasured glance;

looking deep
and deeper still into the sterling beauty of Your fair and gentle
    judgment-face.
I feel the bite of betrayal to my very bones; leaving me here—
alone, without those promised words with which I might again
breathe Your Love.
Lord, you took me captive to this passionate burning
    in my breast,
this affection that claims every waking hour, and demands that
all dreams begin and end with You.
I would surrender again to your abundant Love—a prisoner
    who is
overjoyed with that blessed-bondage.
Then somewhere in the night, beneath this canopy
    of too many witnesses,
I close my eyes—and—
You are—once again—here!
Holding me, absorbed by the splendor of Your presence
    and the promise of
Love yet to come—east of here—somewhere .

ON ADAM'S FIRST VIEW OF EVE

That first summer I sat beneath a pale blue sky,
heavy with the heat of the lazy day, watching
this cotton-cloud drift undetermined, it seemed,
traversing the companionless heavens.
At the far end of this grassy depth stood a sea in motion—
looking icy in the August sun, without any sign of life,
it lived.
Even sparrows seemed disinterested in the hard sun that
laid so great a weight of indifference on my wearied soul.
It came—
Sleep; deep, long, sleep.

Awakened by gentle nudge—
And then—from the far horizon—I saw her small frame
    moving
with such grace across that tepid sea; coming too near
    for my heart
to hold back.
The glow of the day fixed itself all over her, and even
    the sparrows turned
to gaze in disbelief at this beauty rare.
Wondrous place, transformed now by this singular presence.
It must be that she will stay with and within my heart—or
the summer will soon submit to a day without joy.

A GLORIOUS UNFOLDING

What do I see when I *look* at you?
This beach along the coast of Maine, with rocks, strong—
there withstanding the waves of time, yet
tender in their embrace of the ocean's incessant demands;
delightful in making this routine of tides a symphony
    of whisper and
wordless song—singing down through the centuries,
    from God's first
Word.
What do I see when I *gaze* at you?
A pasture washed clean with white rain, radiant with
the children of nature's pallet, colors spectacular with arms
    waving
green against a golden sky.
Tall, silent cedars, watching with care and compassion
    for those
little ones playing in the softness nestled below.
And there, in that green sea of softness one is invited
    to find rest;

a glorious unfolding of your troubled heart—a petal
   for a hand reaches out
to soothe your fevered brow.
What do I see when I *watch* you?
Generations of gracious good will and parental passion;
a smile fashioned through a genuinely gracious heart;
eyes speaking in all that is of life—the lovely
   and the loveless,
yet shining out some gracious benediction to give joy to the
sagging soul.
I watch this marvel of God's own hand—touching life with a
Gracious sweetness.
What do I *hear* in your name spoken softly?
Larks circling an open field, there only to frolic;
a night wind walking the face of this dark earth, wanting to
enfold someone.
A brook bouncing over ageless rocks, making a new song to
ease the sorrows of those aching souls willing to listen.
And love—a lyric sung by angels in some hidden,
   heavenly chamber.

DIVORCE

Late in the day, and alone.
Even though never—finally—alone.
I wish it were as simple as coming home to her
laughter and liquid smile.
I wish it were possible for me to put my hand
there—in her own.
Time will not allow such extravagance.
I sit alone, unable to bear this death-like silence seeping
into my soul.
For another day!
Time, its numerical grin, mocks my sorrow in

not hearing redemption's song—today.
Does she know, in her heart, how richly and deeply I care?
The answer comes on a wisp of wind: "But—to what end?"
This foolish man will never find it in his weak,
ineffectual speech;
never say what is there as soulful longing.
She is, for me, like grace—waiting.
And I have not given her so much as she claims; or she me.
But love is always with indifferent eyes to what is gained
     and lost;
love is that fatal joy without which none will ever
     find freedom.
No,
my poverty of words is matched only by my miserable
     attempts at
understanding that which cannot be understood—love sold
     to the
lowest bidder!
Late and alone, I am, once more, mindful of her face—
and I sigh to see her.

LIFE ABORTED

What sorrow and pain, that agony we often bear, when
in our youthful years we choose to follow this certain
     painful path;
and then must carry deep within our souls this appalling
     sadness for
a lifetime.
It would not be the same if today we were told to choose—
for here, in *this* incredible hour, we would rejoice to embrace
     this life
beating there—where God has given it to us;
this life.

Yet, my grief is prolonged, and the face I see in the smile
     of a stranger's child
cries-out to say—"Remember the life!"
One day I awakened only to realize that the one choice had
changed life—mine—
Irrevocably!
Now I could not dream, or hope, or hold this one—gone.
Another—blessed and grateful to God—God's "Yes!"
But not this one, whose small voice must now sing in some
unseen and sacred choir.
Nothing can cure this open gash in my soul, while my heart
will always hold a place for the one whose eyes I never
beheld beholding a dawn, a duck, a dandelion in drifting dance.
This faith is sometimes all that I can bear.
And the hope—the hope that the small heart has forgiven me.
Even at the risk of great, eternal rejection, I will run, when
next we meet,
beyond the barrier of this time and place, and
I will extend my arms, waiting and watching for the same.
Surely God will wash away the formal disgrace, and my child
     will come
to me—
a mother who had *never* forgotten.
My child will, there, fall into my waiting arms,
and then—blessed song of salvation!
I will feel the warmth and wonder of reconciliation,
     too long delayed.
Then I—this *graced* mother—will make sweet music for my
child's sleep.

IN HER MEMORY

Feeling unusually dark today; missing you
extraordinarily;
this pensive soul wanders about in what amounts to a
wasteland.
There can be little more without you; your voice, your smile,
your fragrance, your hair falling softly over your shoulders.
This world walks by me day-by-day and I could care less about
its sights and sounds, its business and bothersome quibbling.
What I pray for is one quiet moment—with you—
somewhere removed.
But then I know that to be a selfish and thoughtless desire;
one that ignores the tenderness that was your life,
the brightness you
brought to life—untarnished, unqualified by the traps
life tends to
toss our way.
I swear to you my undying devotion, and listen to my own
words,
my own weakened voice—echoing into silence—within.
I turn to my window and dream about a longed for
deliverance—
a day when this ache will find release in the short walk
Home—
to Him—to you—to laughter—to Love's eternal embrace.
Not for now—for now there is this internal war between
my heart and
mere common sense, playing-out the full measure of
life's passion, while that more moderate voice issues a
summons to more serious and cautious action.
There, caught between, I hang suspended.
I remember your more temperate soul, your more restful,
patient,
presence.

I know how each day will feel the same—for now—now.
For now and until that day when my breath is stopped short
  and
my soul soars to its quiet rest.
Until then, apart from you will be all pain—and I will live
  for each
promise of your presence.

AWAKENING DISCIPLE

From His generous face I see myself as never before.
He holds before me, His heart—to lay hold with gentle embrace.
This is the One for whom centuries of verse have been
  penned.
They too, somehow, touched by that same sterling Love,
  sought to look
beyond themselves for words in which to frame such
  Splendor.
Speechless, their pens covered paper with clumsy verse;
ink, spilt like blood on wooden beams—shed in such a
  valiant cause.
Still they cannot—dare not—approach this wondrous thing—
  Shoes off!
Like them I stare in disbelief at the hill now soaked
  in sin's release; the full
torrent of fury from
below—vent on that fragile human frame.
Longingly, my eyes search in memory for His
  features—unbroken;
my greedy ears seek His voice—silenced.
I hunger for every word—once spread like honey.
And yet—hold still!
Forever, I am indebted to such a precious and gracious legacy
  as He has
given to the likes of me.

I will join the historic line of those who will seek to honor
    such Love.
I awaken to His purpose.
In rejoicing I am eternally His—
Death is but the prelude to a promise of passion shared.

THE EUCHARIST

I often feel like Moses before the burning bush;
humbled in the presence of an indescribable glory;
this ground on which I stand is made precious in the presence
of bread-broken and cup-poured-out—all light and love—
before me; and I fear to lift my eyes to look upon such
radiance.
His presence meets my very soul in silence—lifting high
the languishing dream and desire.
I often feel like Saul, suddenly a prince among the people;
not by personal power or force of arms; by but a gracious
choosing of which I had no part—all light and love.
He has loved my life into a priceless treasure.
I often feel like David; crazy and carried-away by the wonder
of—what? Bread and Wine—wordless glory that can only
touch the hem of His holiness.
Author of a hundred psalms can only hang his head
    in reverent shame;
for here, with Him, the heart's strings fall into stillness and
awe.
I cannot cease to surrender, to be surrounded with a
    soft-circle of
Heaven's sensitivity.
I cannot but speak my heart to Him here, and then,
    and always.
God give me wisdom, grace, goodness, and everything that will
form a fountain of never-ending
affection.

God help me to hold Him
precious and forever.

A CHERUB PEERING OVER MY SHOULDER

When the work of the day drifted into a final repose,
I sat and looked-out at the world winding wearily down;
Mozart made his magic-flute in the background, turning
    my tensions
into soft and silent reflections,
with a cherub peering over my shoulder, keeping watch and
whispering a word.
And then, as if by some miracle of grace, I beheld
Your face;
there with a warm and welcoming smile setting
    my heart ablaze
with an undying flame of abiding affection.
Softly it came, something serene and memorable
    to melt away
the troubles of the day.
I offer every thought to the thoughtfulness of You.

EMPTY POCKETS

Sometimes it feels as though my heart had
empty pockets;
nothing I could give would express as brightly
the tender joy I am given at the
mention of Your name.
The mention of Your name and I am rich!
My heart turns itself inside-out and there flows
to You,
all the love life—one life—can hold.
I live and the pockets of my heart are empty—but never
poor.

WHEN SILENCE FALLS

With such engaging smile I am lifted high above the
mourning drudgery; this parade of need and longing
dressed in human garb—faces, some remain—foreign.
In your absence this life is so much—
"much ado about nothing!"
Words and motions and inarticulate groaning;
all come to me, and what I hear beneath are
your words, your voice; and see
there in those eyes, bright—so much life, lived and
living.
When I can no longer bear it I simply breathe in and out
your name.
This world with all of its troubling sounds then washes
clean—
a crystal lake, a full moon, a pathway strewn with
scented petals.
Time together—silent—silence—and then,
when silence falls—
this universe of emotion—shared—silence
falls.

THE KINGDOM OF GOD

There is a Place where roses perfume the air, and
unnumbered flowers beckon lovers, linger;
a Garden of such delight, some will walk for ever.
The swans sway in a crystal lake, a ballet of
infinite beauty, the expression of their Creator's
glory wrapped in graceful motion.
Oaks stand tall, centuries of countless storms etched
deep on their bodies; scarred, yet proud to mimic
    their Master—Scarred—pouring a
generous shade over all who pass beneath their unfurled

cross-like-wings.
Cooing companions of love's gray-glory sing and
serenade from place to place—calling all Kingdom residents to
rejoice in the final-freedom of soul, finding the deepest joy.
The King comes to all, saying:
"Stay with Me, here; look deep into My face; find there that
Love which death cannot destroy."
And then, this—
Beneath a summer moon, hung sympathetically in a
    starless sky—
hung like the sun to illuminate the way—there to offer
    soft radiance
to those He loves.
Lost in His voice; hoping beyond hope to be held
    in His favor
Forever.
They turn their eyes to this wounded Lamb, fleece soaked
    in Love
Divine;
and find they are wrapped in purity and grace.

I RECALL

I wonder if at this very hour you sleep,
dreams walking you through the night, silent;
softly breathing, restful in your soul.
I cannot bring myself to claim the pillow, because
something in my soul is restless, as though I had this
fire burning in my breast.
I can almost reach out to touch your cheek, and how I wish I
could;
just once more feast on your repose.
You are such a marvel to me; I am lost in the universe of
your radiance.
I want to watch you in the night, sleeping—to lean into your

sweet face and whisper.
I recall—
The autumn moon cut a white-hot light—burning
    its presence across
the face of the landscape, looking for
lovers, finding us.
Kicking leaves from the path, we walked.
Just one moment in time—we stood and embraced.
This glorious ritual repeated in the presence of
    a blushing harvest moon.
We were making dreams, while
loving dawn into existence.
I recall—

WITH UNREQUITED LOVE

Now I sit here, caught between what is and what could be,
casting a glance that lands softly on her face—unknown.
I feel such a fool; a coward at this love,
    unwilling to give her the place she rightly deserves;
a place of honor for the graceful soul she is.
Now I sit, grinning like a teen in the presence of desire;
suffocating in the balance of her;
    trying not to show how caught I am—caught and captive.
Charm—charisma—flows from her—a stream of grace and
generosity.
With joy I want to tell her—to
tell her.
I feel my heart sink, with so little to say, to share—like a
simpleton, singing beneath my breath; my soul sinks
    into my
soul—another day.
I bring my meager self into her presence, with nothing
    to give
but the poverty of my words, and
this heart which holds such wealth for her.

The Evening of His Death: For John, the Beloved

Enfolding You in such love,
stellar and widening through the course of eons;
and ever so gently, my love wraps the memory of You.
Silently, unseen—entombed.
I feel Your love like the warmth of the sun—touching
my face.
I hear—I hear Your voice; how precious this heart
now holds You to be in memory—alone.
Startled I sit, gazing into a blue-gray sunset, with
tearful eyes, tracing the horizon—for what?
Perhaps just the silhouette and shadow of Your form,
suspended there in the last light and life of the sun.
Golden hues enfold You, and I breathe the wonder.
As darkness begins to blanket the world, I am
with You—entombed.
Night is falling, with stars, a canopy of splintered-white.
Somewhere a robin dove melody to some other and her voice
breaks the night air with beauty.
And You?
You are that soft breeze that brushes my cheek—that
breeze—breath of life—that wipes my brow.
Blessed moment.

Long, Long Between Us

Long, long the love between us,
Sometimes blinding us to the very light of day;
never diminished.
The flame often grows dim from the
world's windy demands.
From my heart—a thought, a sigh, a sight
unparalleled in the length of days.
The deep pool of your eyes and I swim into that

expressive depth, diving again and again to retrieve
something from your soul—a thought, a sigh, a sight.
This place I hold with you is hallowed ground—
and grace fills the near space between two hearts.

My Shaken Soul is Quieted

It flows with the current of contentment,
far beyond what the heart can hold.
So many dreams pass through my soul and lodge
their pointed-pleasures deep within.
Lost in an ocean of untold, unseen, yet unknown
rapture; I bow my head in silent awe that
God should be so good to me.
When life lingers on the edge of sorrow,
I say the Name, like lighting a candle in a
sacred space;
that Name has healing power and
peace.
My shaken soul is quieted.

Sabbath

Candy bars and chocolate drops;
rainy days in loose sweater and socks;
coffee, fresh and home in overflowing cup;
tucked beneath a blanket.
Here and there the sounds of child-like laughter.
A lasting love, a longing look, a soft embrace and
days—delightful—the joyous discovery of
more.

Why Do You Elude My Longing?

That soft and gentle Word that only He can speak is
silent, as silent as the falling snow.
Warmth evades the chill of my chastened heart, while
I touch the memory of yesterday as mystery and grace.
This tremulous soul looks deep, and deeper still, and there
just there, this passion for life flares like a flame.
Words, words, words—Word !
Why do you elude yearning, the
wonder I feel?
Tears come to my waiting eyes as life longs for life
in Him.
This captive, bound in chains of what was and will
never be—
now that He is silent.

While Sleep Goes Elsewhere

The long shadows of night summon me to enter sleep;
but that one frame of thought—her face and scent—hold
my heart in wakefulness;
while sleep goes elsewhere, to seduce some other.
I am left in this night to stare, as if into a distant future
not far, yet still beyond reason.
That form I see in the peculiar world of phantom images stands
with outstretched arms.
She waits.
Time keeps secret, and rolls on and by, day-by-day.
Soon, sleep will come; then dreams; then daylight—
One day a long love will be the dream shared.

For the Child Lost

Would that I could gift you on this day:
With trees, large, their green canopies to shade you;
with soft meadow and breeze to warm and wash over you;
with wild flower scent and scene of golden maidens—their
dark eyes to charm you;
with angels wings, fanning a whisper of grace and hope
embracing your heart and soul;
with cotton clouds dancing to the song of a robin choir;
with the laughter of other children, merriment to bring you joy;
with moonlight on a summer's night, shimmering above a lake;
with remembrance of your own eternal worth and the Lord's
love for you;
with friends to gather at your birthday cake—to hold,
    to help, to heal, to have;
with blessed beauty to charm and passion's breath touching
    your cheek.
These would I give, and pray God gift me with your presence
    here
Forever.

Maranatha!

Does time need be so cruel?
Moving with such slow and steady rhythm;
touching neither today nor tomorrow;
while my anguished heart sighs with
breathless desire, yearning for nothing so much as
to have Him here—forever.
Am I this fool, caught in a web of lengthened-longing?
Dreaming of a time, a place far removed from this
vacated space;
here with His absence haunting my soul.
Does time need care so little for this longing?

This is love's real need—to embrace Him
forever.
There I can see, just beyond the horizon,
lit bright by yet another sorrowful moon,
a Kingdom that never comes in coming—little
joy in waiting and watching.
Does time need be so insensitive to patience
pushed beyond all reason?
I dream—Him;
I pray—Him;
I yearn—Him;
I ache—Him;
I desire—Him;
Maranatha!
Does time have such a heart to bring Him, here, finally—
Today—tomorrow—forever?

Her Father's Death

It was her father's fall from earth that
dark and painful time her bright star fell;
with tears of sorrow washing her soul,
there her loss called forth love—or some
mystery in her, some tenderness.
I was so close to her and that great hurt which
held her captive, hostage to memories of her father's
touch, his love, his laughter—
his long care.
My soul sang out to her with a feeble prayer to appease
her soul.
At risk of wreckage, I entered her precious space—her
sorrow, her quiet, desperate darkness;
helpless I could not be grace and goodness to her;
holding out some word of comfort.

Now each day I throw my prayer into the mystery and
hope that somehow her father will guide a fool's heart,
to give care to his daughter.
I strain to hear his voice, from time to time and beyond;
to hear—silence.

With Bewilderment

I caught with bewilderment the golds of Autumn dancing
on your auburn hair;
while yellows, deep and bold enfolded your gentle form,
held soft against a field of dancing wheat and clapping corn—
ripe.
I caught with enchanted heart the soft whites and pinks of
Spring,
tending to your gentle eyes hallowing your face,
while soft above clouds gathered for your
crown and doves flew in ballet.
I caught with soothed and joyous soul the warm breeze of
Summer's lush breath,
moving through your hair and over your shoulders—bare.
A watching sun showered his rays and wrapped you in the
green grass where you lay—still.
I caught with breathless wonder the glow of
Winter's fire falling soft,
making the contours of you in shadow and silhouette;
    I blush.
While just beyond snow fell silent and routine, building
    around us
a fortress of soft white, sheltering our passion.

In Praise of their Creator

The water washes over the unsuspecting sand, gathers them
and gracefully bears them out to sea, submerged in silent
    acceptance.
Beneath the surface, unseen, yet seeing all they need,
    two dolphins
do some mysterious and ritualistic dance, a movement
    intended—
in praise of their Creator,
a melody of deepest love echoes; long ages ago etched into
their hearts.
The warm waves caress their shining forms, the colors
    of God's own
pallet radiate from the soft edge of their lives;
while all their neighbors of the deep now draw a reverent
    breath,
breathing out a prayer with praise in it.
Far above the dark depth two gulls glide in search of what
    others
think food; not so.
What they crave is to draw ever closer to their Creator;
    to advance
on heaven itself; even to risk being blinded for all eternity
    by that
blast of holy light.
Bravely they mark their course, setting sail beneath a silent sun,
committed to rise ever higher, compelled to beat their
    wings against
heaven's doors.
Then somewhere near the Son's face, they think better,
    turn, dive;
even they are wise enough to return and take their
rightful place.

Two have been interlocked by a love from somewhere
    beyond them;
they walk within this same world and make their way through
    life,
conscious of what their Creator has given.
They too dance out the dimensions of this incomprehensible
    mystery
in which they have been whisked away, submerged in
    silent acceptance.
The finger of God seems to guide them through this perilous
    path, where
they have danced with others, while their hearts have
    held apart.
And when the unseen courageous of creation have spoken
    the last
syllable, there will still be Love to lead them beyond
    the boundary of
Life.
One day their wings will carry them to Him who always
    had them in
Heart.

Spring Sighs

Spring sighs knowing as she does that somewhere in her realm
there is a bud which cannot yet give birth to leaf or flower.
Not for want of Nature's care, not for want of nurture;
but by some untimely plan, they who never yet knew
    the power of such
a love as this must stand in some shadow, until—
until, when?

So Spring sighs; she possesses life with the unbridled passion
of love; she, the source of the rich savor of that

voice, that smile, that backward glance that marks the
    character of the two
who think and feel and dream and yearn as one.
Spring sighs, touched by this untapped tenderness,
    this flame
of holy desire in a human breast.
Spring sighs to see what cannot be said in any tongue
    or language;
Spring folds a hand over her heart and whispers a gentle wind
    to move
just a wisp of hair—that he might hold in his heart as one
    memory the
promise, the presence.
Spring will not hide her face from this glorious gift, enacted
    in the trembling
souls of these two.
What they have, they hold; never holding fast but in faith.
What is between them is hallowed space—always.
Spring sighs as if to sing their love into existence; as if to
    turn the world into
their home; as if she could
bring them to full-fruit.

Now He Will Watch and Wait

At seventy-five he sits and watches this woman.
He has watched before and before; just
her breathing in the middle of the night, or
the set of her eyes, the contour of her face, the
wave of her hair; her soul,
sagging, soaring, sighing, singing.
He has always watched with her, without her; watched
as one single act of reverent homage.
In his heart he holds her close, not for fear of losing
her;

this too, his deep desire, to tell her of a thousand tender
    thoughts;
each one a jewel, a gem of his own devotion to her—to
her.
This woman he must watch; for whom he holds such
wonder—such soulful passion; all these years.
When alone he comforts himself with thoughts;
where they were, when they were—
a winter night, when the walk took them to a flickering fire;
a summer sun and the sound of gulls gliding high above;
flowers clipped from a neighbor's yard—carried home
    to her,
a price for passion.
Soft rain, wind reshaping the set of her hair, a warm night into
early morning, when all they could do was sigh—
for the peace.
Dreams were built of such blessed moments; and now—
Now he will watch and wait; wait as he has throughout—in
joy;
wait—for the whisper of her loving words;
wait—for the glory of her gentle smile;
wait—for the tenderness of her bountiful eyes;
wait—for the invitation to join hands in graceful embrace;
wait—for the time, when, once again he will—watch.
Watch for the wonder that is his love, his long life;
his luster, his liberty, his lass.
Watch as one single act of reverent jubilation.

The Gardener—A Tribute

Row upon row of green on green, and gold;
every morning, early morning, fingers in dirt;
earth's gift of grace in the waiting, just beneath the
soil; just beneath the crust of brown beauty; just

there, the Gardener pushes seeds into their waiting
beds; each one bedded with some holy benediction.
One Man's heart and soul held against a blinding
sky; blue to hurt your eyes, and yet, He smiles with a
soft turn at the edge of His mouth.
This perfect day holds promise for the planting.
A garden of grace, when touched by the tenderness of
One who loves God's creation with unaltered charm,
    becomes
a small, sacred place.
Standing with back bent against the punishing sun,
    the Gardener
wipes sweat from His brow, turns His eyes to that which
    He loves;
the land, trees, the clear scent of God's sweet-breath
    on the wind.
He beholds what others miss; miss with their busy minds,
    and hearts
too far from the gentleness of God's good earth.
Again the Gardener has tasted the glory of bringing
    life forth from
barrenness;
again the Gardener gifts those He loves with the fruit of His
faithfulness;
Again the Gardener has, in the stillness of His most private
    soul, offered
silent praise to
God;
Again the Gardener has graced us with this Truth:
All worth, all joy, all love, all laughter, all—is gift—is
Grace—is
Life—in care of
the Gardener.

Postscript

THIS WORLD is filled with *mystery*; that dynamic of *mystery* spoken of throughout the Scriptures and evident in Jesus Christ. Not mystery as something to be investigated and in the investigation, better understood; *mystery* as a dynamic demanding the response of reverent awe, fascination, and faithful adoration. So often such mystery escapes us in this post-modern world where we have become all-too-accustomed to embracing the explanations of science and technology, as if their findings were the final, the definitive word on the reality under study. Science and technology are of great value in providing improvements to life on several levels, but of limited value in helping us comprehend and appreciate those aspects of life and this world that cannot be quantified or probed to their depths in a laboratory. There is so much more to life than can be comprehended, even by the most brilliant of human minds; *mystery* can only be apprehended, not comprehended, and by the heart, soul, and spirit—as much as with the mind!

I have discovered pastoral ministry to be one grand journey into the *mystery* of life, and at every conceivable level, from the birth of a child to the last breath taken before that grand and final journey into the presence of the Almighty. It is this *mystery* embedded in life itself that has always been the inspiration for my writing and preaching, and certainly the very substance of the poems collected in this book. Whether one is attempting to speak of that passion of human love for another, or speaking of love for God, such speech can only take shape as metaphor, simile, parable, and poetic language, because *mystery* compels us to such speech. The love of a man for a woman, in the form God intended, is as beautiful in its *mystery* as is the love held in a human heart for the Lord Jesus—and equally as fragile. For me, poetry has been a way in which I could attempt to share with others a select form of life experience—pregnant with *mystery*—when all other forms of expression proved inadequate. And in presenting these poems to the public, I have willingly placed myself in a most vulnerable position; not only because there are those who will, and perhaps with good cause, criticize my attempt at this artistic form as hopelessly inadequate, but more importantly because each poem represents an aspect of my own personal story and my own pastoral heart and soul.

I would pray that this collection of poems would awaken in the reader a renewed appreciation for the *beauty* of faith in a *beautiful* God who continues to paint and word this world into the *mystery* of redemption and promise. God is at the heart of this world's deepest longing and attentive to the deepest yearnings of the human heart and soul; and we can still discover *beauty* in this world because *(God) shines in all that's fair.*

Bibliography

Houston, James. *The Heart's Desire: Satisfying the Hunger of the Soul.* Colorado Springs, Colorado: Navipress Publishing Group, 1996.

Johnson, Luke Timothy. *Scripture & Discernment: Decision Making in the Church.* Nashville: Abingdon Press, 1996.

www.ingramcontent.com/pod-product-compliance
Lightning Source LLC
Chambersburg PA
CBHW071104090426
42737CB00013B/2467